The Surprise

Mom, I brought you home
a surprise from school.
Guess what it is.

Is it a great, big, enormous turnip?

No, Mom, it's not something to eat.

Will it huff and puff and
blow your house down?

No, Lilly, it's not scary.

Will it say FE, FI, FO, FUM?

No, Mom, it can't talk.

Will it turn into a pumpkin at midnight?

No, Jo, it'll be asleep by then!

Will it go *Trip, Trap, Trip, Trap,* over the furniture?

No, Mom, not if we train it.

Now, let me see.
It's not something to eat.
It's not scary.
It can't talk.
It sleeps at night …
and it needs training.

Oh, Mike, it's not one of
those kittens from school, is it?
What a surprise!